A House in the Hedge

Story by Damian Harvey
Pictures by Rebecca Elliott

OXFORD
UNIVERSITY PRESS

"I need a new house," said Hedgehog. "My house is too cold."

4

So Hedgehog went to look for
a new house.
"I like your house, Otter,"
said Hedgehog. "But it is
much too wet."

Hedgehog went
to Rabbit's house.

"I like your house, Rabbit,"
said Hedgehog. "But there is
no room for me."

Then Hedgehog went to
Squirrel's house.
"Your house looks warm,"
said Hedgehog.
"But I cannot live in
a tree."

Hedgehog went to Mole's house next. But Mole's house was much too dark.
"I cannot see in the dark like you," said Hedgehog.

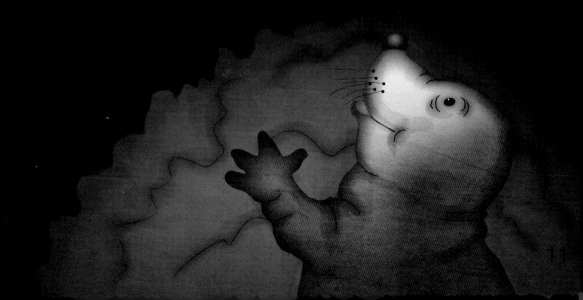

So Hedgehog went back to
his own house. On the way, he
slipped.

Hedgehog rolled
and rolled. He got
covered in leaves.

"I like my house best," said Hedgehog.